First Facts

American Black Bears

by Molly Kolpin

Consultant:
Frank T. van Manen
Research Ecologist
U.S. Geological Survey
Leetown Science Center

CAPSTONE PRESS
a capstone imprint

First Facts is published by Capstone Press,
1710 Roe Crest Drive, North Mankato, Minnesota 56003.
www.mycapstone.com

Library of Congress Cataloging-in-Publication Data
Kolpin, Molly.
American black bears / by Molly Kolpin.
p. cm.— (First facts. Bears)
Includes bibliographical references and index.
Summary: "Discusses American black bears, including their physical features, habitat, range, and life cycle"—Provided by publisher.
ISBN 978-1-4296-6131-7 (library binding)
ISBN 978-1-4296-7183-5 (paperback)
1. Black bear—Juvenile literature. I. Title.
QL737.C27K647 2012
599.78'5—dc22 2011001345

Editorial Credits
Christine Peterson, editor; Kyle Grenz, designer; Laura Manthe, production specialist

Photo Credits
Corel, 9; Creatas, 7, 20; Getty Images: Stone/Riccardo Savi, 13; Newscom: Stock Connection Worldwide/Peter Bisset, 15; Shutterstock: airn, cover, nialat, 5, Thomas O'Neil, 1; SuperStock: age fotostock, 21, All Canada Photos/Don Johnston, 10, All Canada Photos/ Wayne Lynch, 16, imageBROKER, 19

Artistic Effects
Shutterstock: Andrejs Pidjass, basel101658

Essential content terms are **bold** and are defined at the bottom of the spread where they first appear.

Printed in the United States 5410

Table of Contents

All-American Bear

About 900,000 American black bears make their homes in North America. These bears can be 4 to 7 feet (1.2 to 2.1 meters) long. Most adult male bears weigh about 300 pounds (136 kilograms).

Black bears are masters at **surviving** in the wild. Thick fur keeps them warm. Sharp teeth and claws help them find food.

survive—to continue to live

claws

Big Bluffers

Black bears aren't very aggressive. But they can put on a show. When danger is near, they chomp their teeth. They **lunge** forward and swat their huge paws. Sometimes they run toward an enemy in a fake **charge**.

lunge—to move forward quickly and suddenly
charge—to rush at in order to attack

teeth
paws

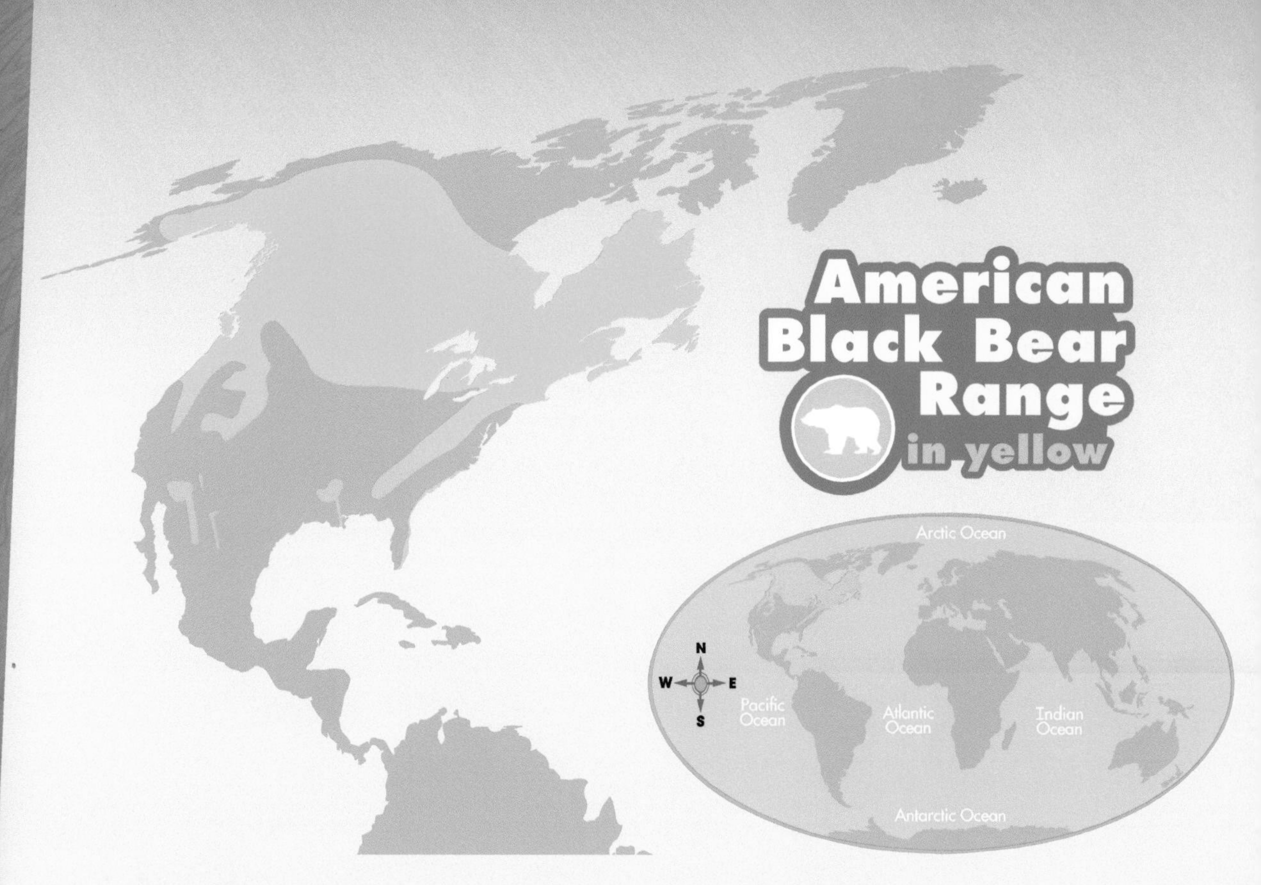

Black Bear Country

Black bears roam the mountains and forests of Canada and the United States. Some black bears live as far south as Mexico. Most black bears spend their time in forests.

Black bears have few enemies. People, mountain lions, and grizzly bears are all threats to black bears.

Fact!
Black bears are the most common type of bear in North America.

Green Eating

Black bears are always looking for a meal. They wander the same trails year after year to find food. The bears search for grass, roots, nuts, and berries. They even climb trees to feed on budding leaves or on nuts.

Fact!
Some trails have been used by bears for hundreds of years.

On the Hunt

Black bears don't just eat plants. They also eat meat. Black bears catch fish from streams and rivers. They hunt young deer. Other times black bears eat eggs from birds' nests. Many black bears use their long tongues to lick up bugs such as ants or bees.

Deep Sleep

In winter black bears **hibernate**. But first they must find a **den**. Most bears sleep in brush piles or hollow logs. Some make dens inside large trees.

Some black bears sleep on the ground. They let snow cover their bodies. The snow acts like a blanket and keeps the bears warm. While sleeping, they live on fat stored in their bodies.

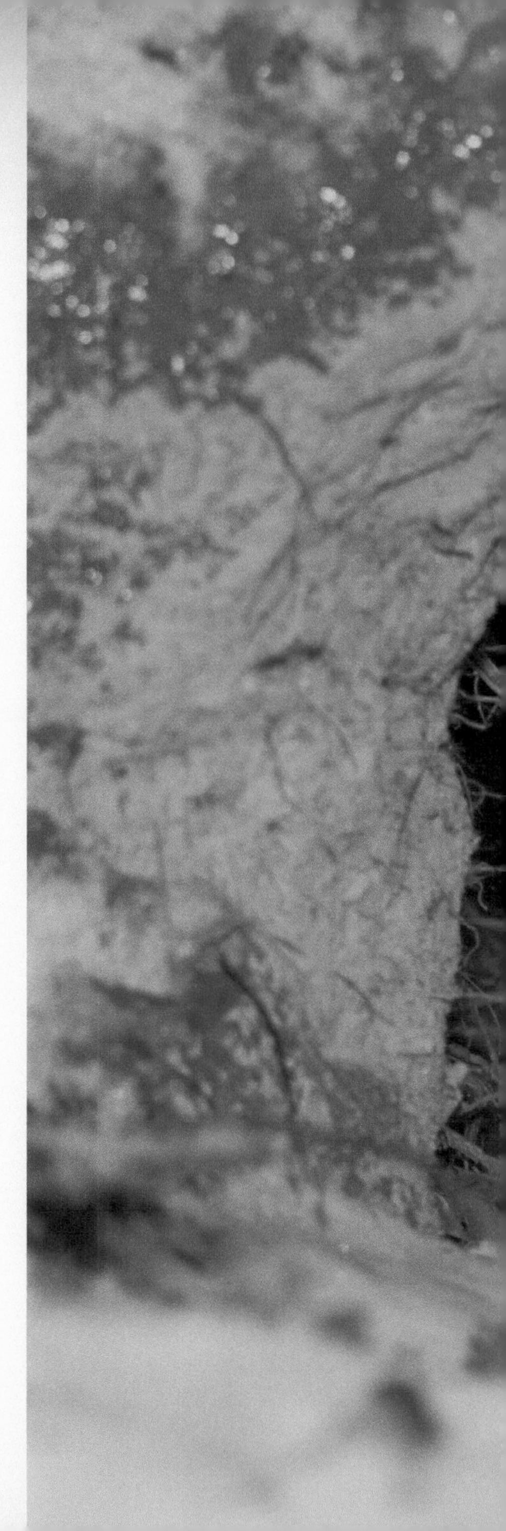

hibernate—to spend the winter in a deep sleep
den—a place where a wild animal lives

Life Cycle of a Black Bear

Newborn—Black bears are blind at birth.

Young—Young black bears stay with their mother for up to 1½ years.

black bear cubs

Adult—Black bears can live to age 25.

In the Beginning

Male and female black bears **mate** in spring. In January or February, the female gives birth to two or three cubs. The mother licks her newborn cubs clean. The cubs snuggle against their mother for warmth.

mate—to join together to produce young

Growing Up

At birth black bear cubs weigh about 12 ounces (340 grams). But they grow quickly. Cubs gain up to 70 pounds (32 kg) in their first six months. Cubs spend their first few months feeding. In spring they leave the den. Their mother teaches them how to find food.

Quick Climbers

Black bear cubs climb trees to escape from enemies. When danger is near, their mother grunts. This sound tells cubs to start climbing.

Amazing but True!

Not all black bears have black fur! Some have brown, blue-gray, and even white fur. Most black bears in the East have black fur. Settlers there were the first to see these bears. They called them black bears, and the name stuck!

Glossary

charge (CHARJ)—to rush at in order to attack

den (DEN)—a place where a wild animal lives

hibernate (HYE-bur-nate)—to spend winter in a deep sleep

lunge (LUHNJ)—to move forward quickly and suddenly

mate (MATE)—to join together to produce young

survive (sur-VIVE)—to continue to live

Read More

Jackson, Tom. *Black Bears*. Nature's Children. Danbury, Conn.: Grolier Scholastic, 2008.

Macken, JoAnn Early. *Black Bears*. Animals that Live in the Forest. Pleasantville, N.Y.: Weekly Reader Pub., 2010.

Shea, Therese. *Bears*. Big Bad Biters. New York: PowerKids Press, 2007.

Internet Sites

FactHound offers a safe, fun way to find Internet sites related to this book. All of the sites on FactHound have been researched by our staff.

Here's all you do:

Visit *www.facthound.com*

Type in this code: 9781429661317

Check out projects, games and lots more at
www.capstonekids.com

Index